# Historic Lindsay

Dedication

To Roy P. Wilson,

Publisher, The Lindsay Daily Post

HISTORIC LINDSAY

by Alan R. Capon

Including a portfolio of
Lindsay Portraits by
John E. Boyd

Mika Publishing
Belleville, Ontario
1974

Cover Picture:

The *Esturion*, owned by the Boyds of Bobcaygeon, made two round trips to Lindsay each day and carried the Royal Mail. Many and varied were the steamboats that plied the waters of the Kawartha Lakes and Scugog River, many of them passenger, excursion and mail carrying types as well as tug boats coaxing long booms of logs to area sawmills.

All rights reserved
Copyright © 1974 Alan R. Capon
Portfolio of portraits copyright
John E. Boyd
Cover drawing copyright C. W. Kettlewell

Mika Publishing
ISBN 0-919302-84-X
Belleville, Ontario
1974

Contents

Introduction	7
From Purdy's Mills to Lindsay	9
Lindsay Pioneer Newspapers saw Sir John A. in different Light	21
How Lindsay reacted to Lincoln's Murder	24
Firewater sunk to Lake Bottom	26
Lindsay's Bloodless Bullfights	27
Lindsay was hit by Railway Fever	31
Saints, Indians and Royalty Provided Names for Streets	37
Time out of Mind	39
The "Glorious Twelfth"	48
Time Capsule in Cornerstone	52
Visit of Billy Sunday	54
Many Newspapers have served Lindsay	55
My Home Town	60
Builder of Railways Founded Hospital	61
Squire McDonnell	63
Getting Back at Col. Sam	65
Bogus Plates Hidden in Walls	68
Mayors of the Town of Lindsay	69
Lindsay Portraits	73

LINDSAY
My Home Town

A PARTIAL VIEW OF KENT STREET, LINDSAY

Song Written For "OLD HOME WEEK"

JUNE 28th TO JULY 5th, 1924

WORDS BY

Introduction

Shortly after my first book "His Faults Lie Gently" was published at Lindsay many persons suggested I prepare a book of stories on the town.

Some of the stories appearing in this book were prepared at that time but the project was never completed because of a move from Lindsay to Picton.

Last year a book of short stories published under the title "Stories of Prince Edward County" sold well and is now available in a second printing. The friendly reception given this book encouraged me to complete "Historic Lindsay".

In the compilation of the book the files of *The Lindsay Daily Post* proved invaluable and the author also expresses his appreciation to librarians Mrs. Janet Nowakowski of Victoria County Library, Moti Tahiliani of Lindsay town Library, Ford Moynes, John E. Boyd, David Walling, A. E. Hick, John Eakins, Mayor David Logan and the late Art Beal for their assistance and encouragement.

The stories range from the early settlement of Lindsay to the infamous bullfight. Lindsay Development Commissioner S. R. Pitts recently recalled that a few years ago he and his wife were visiting Alaska via the inland passage. "I was sitting on the docks at Skagway attempting to read the local paper by the light of the midnight sun when I became engaged in conversation with one of the chaps unloading the ship. Somehow the name Lindsay entered the conversation and he immediately asked 'Isn't that the place they held the big bullfight?' "

Over the years the town of Lindsay has had and continues to have claims to fame through the achievements of her famous sons and daughters; the accomplishments of The Academy Theatre, and the twinning of the city of Lindsay with Nayoro, Japan.

To native sons and adopted sons, Lindsay is to many, in the words of the Old Home Week song of 1924, "My Home Town."

Purdy's Mills plaque

From Purdy's Mills to Lindsay

Over one hundred and fifty years ago, the site on which Lindsay now stands was but a vast, forbidding and unhealthy cedar swamp, and this is how the first settlers on the government reserve found it. The government of Upper Canada first offered land for sale in the area in 1821. It was located in the township of Ops in the Newcastle District.

The settlers built their cabins out of pine logs with the chinks filled with moss and clay. Oiled paper served for windows. Black flies and mosquitoes made work outside torture and at night the howl of wolves could be heard, sometimes by the very doors of the dwellings.

The first settler in Ops Township was Patrick Connell and others joined him along the valley of the Scugog. Just south of the area where the original portion of Riverside Cemetery is situated, a lot was granted to Rev. Father Crowley, the sole Roman Catholic priest in Central Ontario to assist in the settlement of the township. He had come to Canada from Cork, Ireland, with the Robinson immigration. The lot passed in 1846 to his nephew John Ambrose. In the late 1820's the priest had a house built at the water's edge for the storage of settlers' effects and the area is known as Priest's Landing.

The first name of the settlement in the wilderness was Purdy's Mills, after the frame grist and sawmill erected by the Purdy family. William Purdy and his sons Jesse and Hazard entered into a contract with the government in 1827, and the Purdys were to put up a ten-foot dam, build a sawmill in 1828 and a gristmill in 1829.

A few shanties were built for the workmen and Mr. Purdy erected a dwelling for his family that also served to accommodate passers-by, as there was no tavern at the time. Log barns were built with corrals for the stock.

The small village at this time was also known as Portage Village, from the name of a Mississaga camp site located nearby, known as "Onigahning" (The Portage).

After the Purdys built the first dam (completed September, 1828), the spring freshet of 1829 swept it away. The Purdys obtained an extension of time from the government and the new dam was ready in April, 1830.

Another dam was built at Bobcaygeon. The water of the lakes and rivers rose and a fever and plague swept through the settlement, becoming epidemic. There were no doctors around and the settlers had to battle the disease as best they could. So severe was the fever epidemic that Lindsay was sometimes referred to as "the sickliest place in all Canada."

The dam with a head of ten feet was built at the head of some rapids at a point at the foot of what was later Georgian Street. Purdy was also authorized by the government to grist for the settlers for a miller's toll of one-twelfth. Business was brisk and customers sometimes had to wait days for their turn. Customers came from far afield, and it is recorded that a sixteen year old girl carried a bushel of grain fifteen miles to the mill.

An Order-in-Council was granted on May 9th, 1834, to permit Purdy to overflow on certain lots of land without being subjected to any action for damages. Purdy received four hundred acres of land and freedom from legal action by the many settlers upstream whose land would be extensively inundated by the building of the dam.

The water, however, flooded far over the banks of the Scugog River, over East and West Cross Creeks and Scugog Lake, drowning trees and causing fever and ague through stagnant waters and bringing death to some settlers.

In 1838, farmers from as far south as Port Perry picked up their axes, pitchforks and flintlocks and marched to the mill. They hacked down the dam and it swept away. Although an attempt was made at one point to call out the militia, it would appear the settlers' grievances were so genuine that the government took no action against them.

Following an agreement of December 18th, 1843, between Purdy and the Board of Works of the Province of Canada, the Board of Works built a dam and lock further downstream and granted Purdy use of all surplus water that was not needed for navigation.

For his part, Purdy had to keep the dam in repair and relinquish any and all claims for damages from the destruction of his first mill dam in 1838. In settlement for this he received from the government four hundred pounds in cash.

Commenced in 1838, the government dam was completed in 1844. It raised the level of the river by seven feet, three or four feet less than before. The settlers were satisfied, although they complained again several years later when Hiram Bigelow, Purdy's successor, placed a flash-board along the top of the dam raising the water an extra foot.

The lock was built in 1844, opening the river to navigation, early vessels being horse-drawn boats and small barges operated by horse-powered treadmills with side paddle-wheels.

About 1851, steamboats were built with the S.S. *Woodman*, a one hundred-foot side-wheeler of Port Perry, the first to be launched, and the S.S. *Ogemah* of Fenelon Falls the next. Many others soon followed.

Later the lock was abolished because of the cost, and a timber slide was built. The slide gave place to a lock again in 1870.

Notwithstanding the fever and other vicissitudes, the town grew slowly and by the general census of 1852 the village of Lindsay boasted four hundred and fifty souls.

How did the town get its name? This too is lost in the mists of antiquity, but legend has it that a surveyor's assistant or workman named Lindsay, employed by surveyor John Huston of Cavan in 1834, who laid out the town in the swamp, was accidentally shot in the leg. Infection set in and Lindsay died, being buried in the area now known as Mcdonnell Park, near the Scugog River, on or near the site of the present Royal Canadian Legion Hall.

Mr. Huston's survey diary, which is preserved in the Ontario Archives, records his surveying of the land at the request of Mcdonnell of Peterborough and records who he hired and dismissed during 1833-34, but makes no mention of a man named Lindsay. However, the diary is clearly marked "Lindsay" at the top of the first page indicating that the place might already have been known by that name in 1833, although the word Lindsay might have been added to the diary at a later date.

Although the story of the dead surveyor is the most common explanation of the origin of the name, another is that somewhere near the town was located a tavern, owned by a Mr. Lindsay. Settlers were wont to say that they were going to Lindsay's, and this may have eventually been adopted as the town name.

It is possible too that the name was chosen at a time when the post office wanted an official name for the village for postal purposes.

The original area surveyed was bounded by Lindsay, Colborne, Angeline and Durham Streets, about four hundred acres. The area was bisected by two main streets: Kent Street and Victoria Avenue, each one hundred feet wide. On the four corners of the intersection was a six-acre market square known as "Queen's Square", and this area was reserved for future development. The other streets were laid out sixty-six feet in width.

Victoria Avenue was named after the heiress-apparent to the throne, and Kent Street after her father, the Duke of Kent.

It was many years after the town was planned before actual settlers could be induced to purchase even the choicest of corner lots on Kent Street, even at forty dollars, and according to a newspaper report of August, 1874, many were of the opinion that a great mistake had been made in the selection of Lindsay as a place at all suitable for living beings other than bears, wolves and wild cats.

Charles Britton who came to Lindsay in 1837 described the town site as a bog. He claimed that on one occasion he attempted to ascertain the depth of the water and mud on Kent Street and with a pole probed more than twenty feet deep but was unable to strike anything solid.

It is recorded that deer were chased down Kent Street in early days by wolves and that the howl of wolf packs drove terror into the hearts of the settlers.

Early settlers included William Culbert who arrived about 1833, David Ray and Edward Murphy. A store was opened by Major Thomas Murphy in 1834. The post office was established the same year with Major Murphy as postmaster. He was succeeded in this post by Mr. Culbert.

Major Murphy also built a distillery about 1835, and this was located on a creek north of the town known for a long time after as Old Distillery Creek. The distillery apparently closed, partly because the major came to enjoy his own product too much. He later opened another distillery on William Street and there too he was reportedly the best customer.

Views of Town of Lindsay circa 1880.

Another distillery was begun later by Benjamin Stacey, and the town saw the rise and fall of numerous breweries.

The swampy area of town was thick with cedars in the early days. In places they were so dense that, although the water of the

Scugog could be heard rushing by, the river could not be seen for two rods back.

R. McLean Purdy, who was born near Brockville, moved with his family to Lindsay in 1837. He was related to William Purdy. He recorded in 1898 his first view of Lindsay:

The whole place was a tangled mass of cedar and hardwood; but visions of the future were present, and the remaining two hundred acres forming the townsite of to-day were sold in half acre lots at twenty and thirty dollars with five acre park lots at appropriate prices.

About 1834, Jeremiah Britton together with his sons Charles and Wellington came from Port Hope, settled on the Purdy property and erected a log tavern at the corner of Lindsay and Kent Street, East — the first hostelry in the settlement. The tavern was built on an acre lot bought from Purdy for $100. A notice was prominently displayed in the tavern which read "Keep sober or keep away!".

Subsequently, James Hutton started a small store on Kent Street; another early settler was Dominic McBride; a Thomas Sowden from Cavan obtained a store, and a Mr. Fulford started a carding mill. By 1840 the village housed about two hundred people, and half-acre lots on Kent Street were now selling for as high as $100 cash.

Other early residents in the village were James Twohey, Thomas Clarke, Thomas Vane, Nicholas Powell, William Thatcher, Lieut. Logie, R.N., Lieut. C. Moe, R.N., C. Ruttan and W. McDonnell. A few years later Thomas Keenan settled in the village and opened a general store and Hiram Bigelow arrived and built a large stone grist mill.

Wildnerness still surrounded the settlement and wolves could still be seen chasing deer on Main Street. A woman was supposed to have been eaten by bears or other wild animals near the site of the Riverside Cemetery. Only her handkerchief was ever found.

Lindsay has experienced a number of armed invasions in its history. The first came in December, 1837, after Major Thomas Murphy, for some reason, started a rumour in Peterborough that William Lyon Mackenzie was hiding in Lindsay. A column of about three hundred armed men were sent in and several salvoes of musket fire were let off. The men were a detachment of the Peterborough militia under Colonel Alexander McDonnell, searching for Mackenzie.

View of the Lindsay lock around 1890.

Miller William Purdy, who had spoken rather too plainly against the Family Compact and of sympathizing with the Mackenzie Rebellion, was arrested and taken to Cobourg jail. He waited without trial for some time but was at last released and told to return home. Upset by this experience, he moved to Bath with his son Jesse, while his son Hazard remained in charge of the mill.

The second Lindsay invasion occurred in 1838 after the Purdy dam had flooded the surrounding land. The plague and fever, produced by the rotting vegetation, roused the area farmers who gathered together, marched to Lindsay and destroyed part of the dam. In the spring of 1844, Hiram Bigelow bought the mill and the Purdy tract, and Hazard Purdy moved to North Dakota.

The third Lindsay invasion took place on July 12th, 1846, when Billy Parker, a noted Orangeman from South Emily who had been roughed-up in town, returned with a crowd to avenge himself. The townspeople gathered to defend themselves but a deputation met with the visitors and a confrontation was averted.

The final invasion came in the summer of 1847, when Bigelow received permission to put a foot-high line of planks at the top of the dam to raise the water level. When the area farmers learned of this, they marched again with axes and rifles to remove the planking.

Catholic Church and Convent around 1890.

Kent Street had been chopped out by 1840. Other streets followed, and by the time of the general census in 1852 it is reported that Peterborough was getting jealous of Lindsay, the "rising place".

The town was incorporated by an act of the Legislative Assembly, dated June 10, 1857, and shortly afterwards the railroad from Port Hope was completed to the village.

The first town council met in a frame town hall on the northwest corner of Kent Street and Victoria Avenue on July 20th, 1857.

Robert Lang was elected the first mayor; Foster Cain was reeve, and councillors were: William Thornhill, David Brown, Jeremiah O'Leary, J. Healey, H. G. Clarke, James Walsh and J. McCarthy.

The clerk and treasurer was T. A. Hudspeth, and the chief of police was John Douglass.

One of their first decisions was to appoint a committee, consisting of Messrs. O'Leary, Cain and Thornhill, to draft a by-law for the purpose of regulating the sale of "Spiritous Liquors" in the municipality.

Throughout Canada in early days the great curse of the country was the uncontrolled use of liquor. In almost every village and on every crossroad stood wretched taverns, and whiskey flowed freely.

"Though the disaster had almost annihilated Lindsay, yet the inhabitants of the town were in a manner compensated to some extent by the vote for the separations of the counties of Peterboro and Victoria, which took place on the Monday following the great fire," read the review of the town in the Evan's 1877-78 Town Directory.

"Peterborough as usual, was working in opposition to the measure, but this opposition only incited the friends of separation to greater activity. Their exertions were crowned with success, and Lindsay established as the chief town of the County of Victoria," stated the *Canadian Post*.

A Crimean veteran, Samuel Tucker of Durham Street, recalled in a newspaper article written in 1912 that the fire had swept the town one year before he moved to Lindsay. He said the town was still mostly a mass of charred remains, especially in the East Ward where he remembered only a few houses remaining, among which was an old beer house. He said the area of Victoria Park was, at the time of the fire, a dank woody swamp.

The fire spurred the construction of many fine brick buildings to replace the wooden structures which had been consumed.

The town hall and market house were built of brick in 1863 at a cost of $3,600; the high school of brick was erected in 1858 at a cost of $4,000; a separate school house of white brick was built in 1869 at about $4,000; the Loretto Convent of white brick opened in 1874 at a cost, including grounds, of $50,000. The old brick Ops township hall which once stood at the entrance to the Riverside Cemetery was erected in 1860 and, at the time, was considered an impressive structure.

A writer in a directory of the United Counties of Peterborough and Victoria, published in 1858 in Peterborough by T. & R. White, Printers and Stationers, was not impressed by Lindsay's growth:

> *For its age it cannot boast the size some would naturally expect from the richness of the surrounding country.*
>
> *But for many years it laboured under disadvantages which even its enterprising inhabitants could not combat — in the shape of bad roads and the consequent difficulty of access to the seaboard.*
>
> *But this is an age of Railroads, and the iron horse has within a few short months changed the aspect of Lindsay as well as other places.*

The 1858 directory records Lindsay as having a population of nearly two thousand and states:
> *It also possesses an excellent waterpower, on which are mills both for gristing, and manufacturing lumber; one bank (an agency of Upper Canada), four or five excellent hotels, two foundries, two tanneries, mechanics and operatives of all description and callings; about fifteen or twenty stores and shops, where every article, whether for use, ornament or comfort, can be obtained as easily and reasonably as in a frontier town.*

The report further notes that the soil, on the score of fertility, easiness of culture and mineral promise could not be surpassed. At this time four steamers plyed between Lindsay and Peterborough. Fish and game were also reported as plentiful.

The 1858 directory lists T. R. Adams as the postmaster; Dr. John Allanby as a surgeon on St. Paul Street; Charles Britton, merchant; S. & O. Bigelow, merchants; Patrick Carew, innkeeper; Thomas Donnely, innkeeper; Hartley Dunsford, registrar; Joseph Funk, innkeeper; E. D. Hand, publisher of *The Advocate*; B. F. Jewett, innkeeper; Keenan and Lenihan, merchants; George Kempt, lumber merchant; Anthony Lacourse, barrister; Robert Lang, mill owner; Alexander M'Cauly, lumber merchant; Jeremiah M'Carthy, chair and cabinetmaker; James M'Kibbon, mayor; William Silverwood, grocer; Henry J. Waite, proprietor *Victoria Herald*; Hugh Workman, livery stable keeper.

Many of these names wend their way through the early history of the Town of Lindsay, and the descendants of some live there today.

Lindsay Pioneer Newspapers saw Sir John A. in different Light

Sir John A. Macdonald, architect of Canadian Confederation, visited Lindsay on two occasions. Once as prime minister, and later as leader of the opposition.

Although few records seem to exist today on his first visit in 1872 or 1874 when he spoke from the balcony of the opera house, now the Lindsay town hall, a number of documentary records remain extant on his visit to the town on Wednesday, September 12, 1877, for a "Grand Conservative Demonstration".

Advertisements in the town papers of the day record that special trains from Port Hope were arranged, one bringing Sir John A. to the town. The train connected with specials at Millbrook and Peterborough.

Another special train ran from Orillia, connecting at Woodville junction, on the Toronto and Nipissing railway. There also was a special from Whitby, and, on the Victoria railway, from Kinmount.

The result of his visit was either an enormous success or a dismal failure, depending upon in which newspaper you read the report. At that time Lindsay had two newspapers, the ultra-Tory weekly *The Victoria Warder* and the ultra-Grit weekly *The Canadian Post*. The billingsgate exchanged by the editors of these two newspapers on political matters of the day was probably unique in the annals of Canadian journalism.

According to the *Victoria Warder*, between 8,000 and 9,000 persons attended the grand demonstration. Not so, said the *Canadian Post* which estimated the attendance at 1,500 persons.
The *Warder* insisted it was a "red letter day" for Victoria County and in replying to the *Post* said:

> *The Post puts the number at 1,500 but our contemporary must be very well aware such a statement is an error. One of the best evidences of the success of the occasion was the worthy leader (editorial) of our contemporary's columns*

last week, every line of which betrayed the attempt to belittle it. But it was futile.

The *Warder* described the parade in the evening in these words:

In the evening a grand torchlight procession carrying a number of transparencies through the principal streets took place led by a band.

But that was not how the liberal *Post* saw the parade. They wrote:

... The thirteen enthusiasts with a whistle for a band and a cent candle for a torchlight procession ...

The *Canadian Post* reaction to the visit of the chieftain was that "There was no spring to it ... the 'tidal wave' did not rise ... the 'tornado' did not go forth to sweep the country ... not even a 'blizzard' of decent energy could be got up for the occasion ..."

They continued: "The whole thing was flat, stale and unprofitable."

The *Warder* attacked back the following week when they wrote in their editorial "saying that the whole thing was 'stale, and flat and unprofitable' is about as pointed an assertion as the reason given by the man why he did not like iced soda water was because he could not bear hot drinks."

Other reports record that a great procession of carriages met the train from Port Hope and conveyed Sir John A. Macdonald and other dignitaries from the station to the drill shed grounds where at a banquet "no less than twelve tables groaned under the weight of a sumptuous repast provided by the caterer, Mr. Geo. S. Sterling." It was reported five hundred - six hundred attended the banquet, although no indication was given of the size of these tables.

Many were the dignitaries present, and local ones included A. McQuade, M.P., Duncan McRae, MPP, Warden William L. Russell, who was reeve of Lindsay, and mayor Thomas W. Poole of Lindsay.

The address of welcome was read by John Dobson, president of the Liberal Conservative Association of the county of Victoria, in which he compared the "wise and statesmanlike course" of Sir John A. in office, with that of the "do-nothing policy of the present government."

"Kent Street, Lindsay, from one end to the other, presented a bright and animated appearance for the arrival of Sir John A.," noted an observer at the scene, "with its fine blocks of buildings, gaily decorated with flags, streamers and bunting. Three very fine arches of evergreens were formed at the intersection of Lindsay, William, Cambridge and Kent Streets."

Sir John A. Macdonald stayed overnight with his friend Mr. Dobson. He left very early next morning for Toronto by train on the Whitby and Lindsay Railways.

The first prime minister, who was seemingly crushed by an electoral defeat in 1873, survived the hot-blooded politics of the time to regain the nation's leadership in 1878, the year after his visit to Lindsay. He remained as prime minister until his death in 1891, only a few months after his final campaign.

The present Town Hall was at one time the Opera House.

How Lindsay reacted to Lincoln's Murder

It is more than one hundred years since Abraham Lincoln died and it is interesting to take a look at how one small Canadian town observed the day of Lincoln's funeral.

In Lindsay, the stores and schools closed, flags were put at half-mast, and a retired British naval officer named Rodden fired off a memorial salute with two small cannons.

In April, 1865, Canadian newspapers were carrying the news of the surrender of Lee's army. It was the beginning of the end of the war as General Robert E. Lee and the entire Confederate army of Northern Virginia capitulated.

Lindsay citizens turning to the news of the Civil War in their weekly newspapers the week of April 21, noted with horror the assassination of President Lincoln. The murder was reported in detail with column rules turned upside down to provide heavy black lines between the stories.

Wrote one editor:

Ever since the dreadful event, it has been almost the sole subject of conversation, and the greatest indignation has been expressed at the foul outrage.

Lindsay Mayor A. Lacourse issued a proclamation requesting merchants to close their shops on April 17th between the hours of 12 and 2 p.m.:

Promptly to the minute, every place in town was closed; the country offices were vacated, the bell solemnly tolled and minute guns fired. The trains on the Port Hope, Lindsay and Bancroft Railroad were draped in mourning.

Noted a local writer at the time:

No event which has occurred for several years so powerfully moved the popular heart; everyone felt that the loss of honest Abraham Lincoln at the present time was a terrible calamity.

The Lindsay papers quoted the *Hamilton Times* report on the closing of the U.S. border to prevent Lincoln's assassin escaping to Canada. No trains were allowed across the border and all passengers received close scrutiny before they were allowed to cross the suspension bridge.

Later, the town newspapers recorded that the parties implicated in the murder were in custody, and stated that the assassin, J. Wilkes Booth, had been shot.

Long Ago...

Circus day about 1890 on Main Street. (Photo from glass plate negative owned by the Polito Bros.)

Firewater sunk to Lake Bottom

Itinerant Methodist missionaries worked hard to bring the Gospel to the Indians in early days, and early in January, 1827, saddleback missionary Peter Jones visited the Schoogog (or Scugog) Indians.

He found an encampment of about forty in Darlington Township that appeared to be receptive to religious instruction. He taught them the Lord's prayer and the ten commandments before he left on his circuit.

The next month he found a number of the same tribe at Whitby and also taught them the Lord's prayer and its meaning and the ten commandments.

As in other places, however, the worst enemy of the Indians was the white trader, and the traders hated the work of the missionaries.

Two white traders attempted to trade with the Scugog Indians for furs a short time after the latters "conversion". They hoped to make the Indians drunk first, and then buy the furs with more whiskey.

They were unsuccessful in their attempts. After getting one or two of the band drunk, the Christian Indians in a body, demanded the whiskey, saying they would not otherwise trade.

Because they wanted the furs, the traders agreed, but were startled to see the Indians cut a hole in the ice, attach weights to the barrels and sink the whiskey to the bottom of Scugog Lake.

"A pleasant incident of the firmness of the Indians, and a base illustration of the covetousness of the white traders", wrote an early Methodist minister.

The Directory of the United Counties of Peterborough and Victoria for 1858 published by T. & R. White, Peterborough records that the Rice Lake and Scugog Lake Indians were both christianized; adopting the Methodist form of belief. It noted that the Scugog Lake Band of Mississaugas had dwindled since 1844 from ninety-six to sixty-one, with only twelve children of an age to go to school.

Lindsay's Bloodless Bullfights

In August, 1958, the Town of Lindsay held a bloodless bullfight that turned out to be a matador's nightmare.

When mention was first made of a bullfight for Lindsay, most people thought it was just a joke, but the committee from the Chamber of Commerce was in dead earnest and Canada's first bullfight was planned.

Matadors were to use wooden swords to support their capes, and the event turned out to be a nightmare for both matadors and promoters.

The bullfights raised the ire of the nation and hundreds of letters of protest poured into the town from across Canada and the United States. Only a few were in favour of the fight.

"We decided to ignore the protests and hope for the best", said Mayor Lloyd Burrows, "and we are hoping, like everyone else, that nothing happens, because if it does, Lindsay would receive a black eye it would never recover from."

Representatives of the Chamber of Commerce flew to Mexico to make arrangements but balked at the price of the bulls. They settled on some relatively inexpensive ones only to experience considerable difficulty in getting the animals passed through customs at the Mexican-United States border.

Another calculation that went awry was the belief by the promoters that the cooler Canadian climate would slow the bulls down, but, in fact, the climate appeared to stimulate the animals. When the bulls, ranging in age from three to five years, arrived they left the truck like "greased lightning" after their gruelling 2,300-mile trip.

The spryness of the snorting seven hundred-pound bulls left the officials worried over the safety of the matadors. Lindsay's bulls looked ready for battle and dangerous and the matadors only had small wooden swords, intended for a symbolic kill. Strict safety measures were taken to safeguard the bulls because officials feared that some crank might try and harm them before the show.

The first show was held in the evening of August 22nd. Lindsay's Plaza de Toros was packed and two male matadors, Gilberto Azcona and Jorge Luis Bernal, and a woman matador, Miss Elizabeth Bilboa, were ready.

Excitement grew in the town; a street parade with bands along the main street promoted the carnival atmosphere and at eight p.m. a stage show commenced. A great hush then fell over the crowd as the time approached for the first of the three bullfights.

The matadors were ready in their suits-of-lights, their pigtails were fastened, their magenta capes swirled and their black hats perched on their heads.

The bullfights were ready to begin.

Stan Pitts, left, with bullfighters Gilberto Azcona and Jorge Luis Bernal. Centre is Bob Mark and right, Dave Thomson.

The toril doors opened and the matadors could see the wicked horns on the beast, but, instead of plunging into the arena as it should, this bull was a Ferdinand, it just stood placidly and refused to be drawn. The crowd hooted and roared and some Toronto press men rushed to the telephones to tell the story of the bull that would not fight.

The next problem was to get the bull out of the ring as the animal was not to be killed. It took a sweet little heifer to get the cowardly bull to leave. Then came the second bull, fighting mad! This time the matador heard the crowd cheer as he stepped out with his cape. The cape flashed, the matador pivoted, the crowd went wild; the bullfight was on.

At one point a floundering bull stepped on the woman matador's capes. It appeared as though she was frozen to the spot as the bull charged. The sand was so deep in the ring the fighters could not get a proper footing.

Lindsay's "bloodless bullfight" was well attended but was a financial disaster. (Photo by John E. Boyd).

After the ceremonial thrust with the wooden sword another problem had to be faced. How did one get a maddened bull out of the bullring if one did not kill him?

Lindsay's police chief at the time, John Hunter, having had some farm experience, said he could get the bull out and strode confidently out to the bull — the animal charged and the chief ran.

With an amazing burst of speed for so burly a man, the police chief reached the shoulder-high barrera at the other side of the arena reaching safety in the nick of time.

Saturday afternoon, crowds again attended the second bullfight and again difficulty was experienced in removing the bulls so that they could be trucked to a Toronto packing plant for slaughter.

Lindsay's famous bullfights lost the promoters a lot of money, due in part to the fact that hundreds managed to get in without paying.

It was to be Lindsay's first and last fiesta brava.

The Canadian National Railway passenger station at one time had well-kept grounds.

Lindsay Hit by Railway Fever

At the end of the last century, small towns across Ontario dreamed of the growth and greatness their communities would enjoy if they could get railways running through, and many communities helped finance the short lines that wandered all over the countryside by the 1870s-1880s.

Railway fever hit Lindsay, and among the first lines planned was the fifty-five-mile Victoria railway from Lindsay to Haliburton. This was later to be absorbed into the Grand Trunk system together with many other local lines, from the twenty-six-mile Whitby, Port Perry and Lindsay railway to the seventy-eight-mile Toronto and Nipissing railway which stretched from Toronto to Coboconk.

In 1874 George Laidlaw, who was born in Scotland and had visited Australia and Canada, proposed a railroad into the Haliburton highlands, where a dozen or so years earlier a British colonization venture, the Canadian Land and Emigration Company, was attempting to populate ten townships (403,000 acres of crown land). Unfortunately, the settlers did not stay in that wilderness of rock and water, that bears the name of a leading member of the company, Thomas Chandler Haliburton (of Sam Slick fame).

Laidlaw bought a ranch in Bexley, on Balsam Lake, to which he retired in 1881. At his death an obituary noted: "One of the epoch-making men in the commercial growth of Canada, . . . he came out of his railway enterprises a poor man."

Laidlaw's plan was to bring in the railways and immigrants together. From this suggestion started the Fenelon Falls Railway Company, incorporated on February 15th, 1871, originally for a line of fourteen miles from Lindsay to Fenelon Falls.

On March 22nd, 1872, the company became the Lindsay, Fenelon Falls and Ottawa River Valley Railway with the idea of a one hundred and sixty-three mile line to the mouth of the Mattawa River, east of Lake Nipissing.

The S. C. Wood, built circa 1877 on trestle north of Kinmount. This was the only locomotive of the Victoria Railway. (From photograph supplied to the National Archives by Charles Heels of Lindsay.)

A Grand Trunk engine rode up on top of a snow plow on Victoria Avenue around 1890. (Picture from Polito Brothers' collection.)

By this time the original idea of transporting immigrants into the emigration society's lands north had been changed to one of developing the iron-ore bodies and other mineral wealth believed to be in the Haliburton area and to export timber from the great pine forests.

The name was again changed in March, 1873, to the Victoria Railway Company and the first sod was turned on August 5th, 1874, by the Hon. C. F. Fraser, commissioner of public works. The Hon. Oliver Mowat, attorney-general of Ontario, gave the keynote speech.

A colony of Icelandic people, three hundred men, women and children, were settled in Kinmount in 1874 to help with the construction work on the railway. They finally migrated to Manitoba in a body in September, 1875.

First proposed as a narrow gauge line, the railway was built standard gauge of four feet eight and a half inches.

Two people to become famous later in railroad lore in Canada were to begin their careers on the Victoria railway; they were chief engineer James Ross, later a Montreal millionaire, and William Mackenzie.

It took some years to complete the thirty-three miles from Lindsay to Kinmount, and to cross the Fenelon River cost $20,000. The builders encountered a giant morass or "sink-hole" four miles north of Kinmount and thousands of freight car loads of ties, trees and earth were poured in before is was crossed.

Steel reached Kinmount in October, 1876, but further building was held up through lack of funds. In 1877, Laidlaw obtained a grant of $8,000 per mile from the provincial government and a bonus of $3,000 per mile from the Canadian Land and Emigration Company for the rails that ran through its lands in Haliburton county. The railway was not to reach the village of Haliburton until November 23rd, 1878, there to stop, for no mineral wealth of consequence was to be found in the area.

Later attempts to carry the railway beyond Haliburton were made but none were ever successful.

The building of the railroads brought troubles to the villages through drunkeness as this report from an early county paper of October, 1876, reveals:

Our village is still growing and improving in appearance, good substantial buildings are taking the place of the old and dilapidated, and business is increasing. Owing to the

> *number of men employed on the V.R.R. what we seem to want at present is a constable, a lockup and a J.P. to dispose of the cases of drunkeness, of which I am sorry to say we have had a great many lately. As a community we are pretty sober, but the railway hands get drunk on pay day, and they stay around the village, corrupting the morals of the young and annoying the citizens generally with their filthy conversation.*

On November 2, 1876, a contemporary report noted that

> *Bunkers (presumably a hotel) has been as full as it could hold and today the station is being raised, the turn-table is being put down. Crego's bridge is finished and an engine has been up here ... the regular train will leave here at nine every morning for Lindsay. We are in high hope, and everything looks bright. Lots of money, plenty of employment, and joy and mirth prevails.*

On November 2, 1876, a report is carried of the formal opening of the line.

> *The iron horse paid the first visit to Kinmount on Monday last, and we learn that the line will be formally opened on Thursday, 9th. A large number of capitalists, cabinet ministers, members of parliament and railwaymen will no doubt enjoy the first trip over the line.*
>
> *... On the arrival of a special from Toronto, a train will start for Kinmount where lunch will be provided, returning to Lindsay where a banquet will be given.*

The total cost of the railway was $880,000 of which $488,000 was to come from public funds. Some difficulty had been experienced before the line could be continued from Kinmount to Haliburton village.

The residents of the townships of Haliburton were naturally anxious to have the railway completed to Haliburton village and indicated that they were willing to support the railroad with a substantial bonus.

Haliburton was then part of Peterborough County, and the county refused the tax request from Haliburton, so the settlers agitated for separation from Peterborough. They were successful and an act was passed establishing the provisional county of Haliburton in 1874, and the county has remained a provisional one to this day. It has never received full county privileges and for provincial and federal elections remains part of Victoria County which

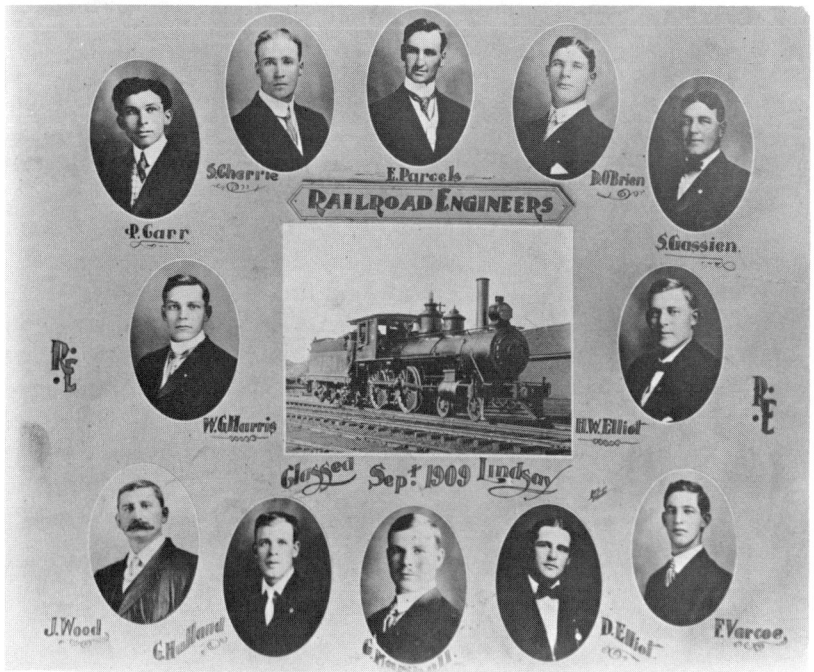
Railroad engineers

also provides administration of justice at the higher levels. The provisional county did have its own county council, however.

The new county at once promised $55,000 to the railway and on November 23rd, 1878 (being formally opened on November 26th), the line arrived in Haliburton, a boon to the settlers and merchants but a financial burden to the county for years to come. The Victoria Railway did not bring the anticipated instant prosperity to the Haliburton area. In fact, it made it easier for dissatisfied settlers to move out and many emigrated west.

Earlier, in 1868, it had been proposed that a "wooden railway" be built from Bobcaygeon to Kinmount to open up the country and create trade, but this had come to naught.

Haliburton County in later years was to become a tourist area, and a Haliburton newspaper correspondent of the day was prophetic when he or she wrote in the *Bobcaygeon Independent* in August, 1878: "A considerable number of visitors are taking their summer vacations here", and added, "it is probable that we shall next season rank as one of the leading summer resorts."

On October 18th, the same correspondent reports on the local scene:

Haliburton is very lively. Lots of fun. We have had as many as twelve navvies in the lockup in one week. The magistrates keep a stiff hand in these matters, arguing that it is just as well for the township to have the money as the tavernkeepers, and they fine them right royally.

The old wood-burning locomotive consumed a great number of logs on its journey and at times the crew (and sometimes the passengers) had to help cut extra wood for fuel on the way.

The Victoria Railway's most successful year was in 1880, when it carried 74,660 tons of freight and 68,390 passengers, earning $83,580. Operating expenses were $55,210.

The Midland Railway of Canada gained controlling interest of the Victoria Railway in 1881, and its one and only engine, the *S.C. Wood*, became No. 86 on the Midland Railway of Canada.

Three Lindsay children look at Canadian National Northern locomotive No. 6218 during a railfan trip to town. The mighty steamer recalls the days when Lindsay was an important railway town. (Photo by Alan R. Capon.)

Saints, Indians and Royalty Provided Names for Streets

One of the streets in Lindsay, Glenelg Street, can be spelled forward and backward and it reads the same. The street was originally named after Baron Glenelg, the British colonial secretary 1835 to 1839.

Many of Lindsay's streets have names of royalty or of famous British statesmen and governors, a few are named after saints, and some for Lindsay people with Canadian or Indian names.

Victoria Avenue was named after the then heiress-apparent to the throne and Kent Street was named after her father, the Duke of Kent. The area north and south of Kent between Cambridge and Sussex Streets was a six-acre market square known as Queen's Square in the early plans of Lindsay.

The original area surveyed was bounded by Lindsay, Colborne, Angeline and Durham Streets. The area was bisected by two main streets, Kent Street and Victoria Avenue, each one hundred feet wide and each meant to be the main thoroughfare. Kent is still the town's main street, but Victoria Avenue was bisected by the railway at a time when towns would do almost anything to get the rails laid into their area.

Other streets laid out in the original town survey were planned at sixty-six feet wide. Those running north and south were named, in the main, after the uncles of Victoria, the Duke of York, King William IV, the Duke of Cambridge, the Duke of Sussex. Another was named Alfred after Prince Alfred but was later renamed Angeline Street.

Albert Street was named after the Prince Consort, and Adelaide Street after Victoria's aunt, the wife of William IV.

Streets running east and west were named after English statesmen and governors of Canada: the Earl of Durham (Governor General 1837, he presented the famous Durham report to parliament. This laid down the principle of colonial self-government);

Lord Melbourne (Queen Victoria's first premier 1833); Lord Glenelg (Secretary of State for the Colonies 1835-39); Lord John Russell (author of the Act of Union and twice prime minister); Sir Robert Peel (British prime minister 1834); the Duke of Wellington (famous British general and premier 1828-30); Sir Francis Bond Head (Lieutenant-Governor, Upper Canada); and Sir John Colborne (Lieutenant Governor, 1828-35).

All the streets named after saints, St. Paul, St. Patrick, St. Peter, St. David, St. George and St. James, are located in the east ward, except one, St. Lawrence Street.

Although Kent is the chief downtown street, once the town had a Main Street, but it does not appear on the latest maps.

Some streets in town were named after local celebrities, Lindsay Street after the surveyor who allegedly had the town named after him, Denniston Street after a lawyer who once lived here, Crandall Street after Capt. Crandall whose steamboats plied the Scugog River, and Logie, after a Capt. Logie.

Sioux and Huron Streets were named after Indian tribes, and a few others have plain names such as John and Bertie, and a few feminine names such as Mary, Jane and Caroline.

To add a final royal touch, the town has King, Queen and Duke Streets, and it is situated in the County of Victoria.

Lindsay also once had a curious little street named Cross Lane but this also seems to have disappeared from the town map.

Main Street although wide, was unpaved.

Time out of Mind

Linday's first fire engine was reportedly the finest fire truck in the province when it was bought in September, 1861, but some citizens felt the cost of $2,000 was too much for the taxpayers of the day.

The engine was built by William Perry of Montreal and the paintings and brass fittings were of the finest description. The fire engine had taken first prize at the Prince of Wales Exhibition in Montreal.

Reported a Lindsay newspaper: "Altogether it is a beautiful piece of workmanship, too beautiful indeed. It will cost the town $2,000. This is a large sum for one engine, reel and hose. We are always in favour of a dear, good article in preference to a poor, cheap one. But in this case we are speaking the sentiments of nine tenths of our ratepayers when we say that to purchase an engine with about $500 of extra work in the way of unlimited brass and beautiful paintings is imprudent, to say the least of it, bearing in mind the heavy burdens the town will have to face during the coming years."

Earlier, in July of that same year, a great fire had laid nearly the whole town in ashes.

The fire engine received a trial in Lindsay in September, 1861, when firemen from Port Hope under the command of Superintendent Williams of the Port Hope, Lindsay and Beaverton Railway brought their engines *Rescue* and *Victoria* to compete against Lindsay's *Cataract*.

Lindsay residents were jubilant when their new fire engine won, throwing a jet of water one hundred and ninety-eight feet, or about twenty feet more than either of the Port Hope engines. The builder had promised that his engine would throw at least one hundred and seventy feet, but trials showed it would throw much further.

* * *

Railways must have presented a pleasing sight in 1887. A report dated September 3rd states that "the cars which run between Lindsay and Haliburton have been painted and titivated, and are now as good as new to look at. The colour is red, with black, yellow and lemon trimmings, the effect of the combination is very good. The engine has also been overhauled and put in first class working order."

* * *

The *Canadian Post*, April 21st, 1871 records the arrest and sentencing to jail of a nine-year old boy with a mania for pilfering. Known as "muskrat", the boy stole a half-a-plug of tobacco from another prisoner while awaiting his trial.

The newspaper also recorded that "an irresponsible piece of whiskey-soaked humanity was rail-fence-surveying on Kent Street about seven o'clock on Monday evening last. He was suffering from a bad attack of the 'blind staggers', which translated means he was 'beastly drunk', and in consequence was staggering along, dodging posts and boxes, in a rather comical manner. The poor fool was more to be pitied than laughed at."

* * *

Years before Lindsay had any street lighting, the then town band members used lighted torches on their caps when they were on parade or giving concerts.

This presumably dangerous method of illumination enabled members of the band to read their music.

One night the band was giving a concert at the foot of Kent Street when a bandsman's hat accidentally fell from his head.

Standing by was an eminent member of the town who was listening to the music. He had long flowing whiskers and when the torch-equipped cap fell, it ignited his beard, causing a great flurry of excitement.

It is recorded that the oldtimers' whiskers disappeared like magic, unfortunately severely burning the old gentleman.

* * *

It is recorded that 16.2 inches of snow fell on March 28th, 1876, isolating the town of Lindsay for nearly two weeks. So much snow fell that by the time the merchants shovelled it off the walks onto the road, the roadway was piled so high that it was impossible for anyone to pass.

On March 1st, 1904 a tremendous snowstorm took place and every available engine and snowplow was sent out to attempt to clear rail lines and roads.

An oldtimer named McColl who lived in Fenelon Falls decided that day to drive his team to Lindsay. The snow was very deep but there was a heavy crust on the surface. As he proceeded on his way, he noticed what appeared to be a bottle of whiskey embedded in the snow with the neck of the bottle sticking out. He left his cart and attempted to pull the object from the snow but it held fast.

Investigating further he found that it was a glass insulator on top of a telegraph pole.

* * *

Navigation on the Scugog River in 1871 was active and a newspaper of April 14, 1871 reports that Capt. Crandall of Lindsay was building three new scows of the capacity of 130,000 feet each. This gave him a total of twenty-six scows and four steamers in operation. His steamers plying the Scugog at the time were the *Sampson,* the *Commodore,* the *Champion* and the *Ranger.* Crandall Street is named after the Captain.

The first high school in Lindsay was built in 1889 at a cost of $27,000. A report of the opening ceremonies published January 26th, 1889, stated that the new collegiate institute was formally opened the previous Tuesday "with much eclat." The report continued: "It is a substantial and handsome red brick structure, three stories high containing six large classrooms of which six are now in use." The contract price was $21,800, but when the heating plant and ventilating system was added, the total cost rose to $27-000. The new collegiate was opened by the Hon. G. W. Ross, Minister of Labour, and Adam Hudspeth, M.P., who was also chairman of the school board.

* * *

In the Lindsay, Victoria, Haliburton and Peterborough areas, the Trent Canal was frequently referred to as "Sam's Ditch" as it was a pet project of long-time Victoria-Haliburton member of parliament, Lt.-Gen. Sir Sam Hughes.

* * *

A story in the *Victoria Warder* of November 2nd, 1876 describes a case of careless driving. "On Friday afternoon a man driving a pair of horses round the corner from George Street onto Hunter Street eastward knocked down a little boy who was passing

During the first World War the F. R. Wilford Shell Factory in Lindsay turned out shells by the thousands. This picture was taken about 1915-16. Named on the back of the photograph: Jack Zangsinger, head mechanic; Casey Jones, Bert Mason, Howard Galley, Louis Smith, Bob Hamilton, Charles Saunders, Earl Beadle, Jack Starke, Wentworth Sedgewick, Charles Alexander, Sam Johnston and Arthur Sedden.

along the crossing. He was not much hurt. The driver proceeded on without even waiting to see if he had done any mischief by his culpable negligence. The careless inattention of many drivers is extremely blamable, and deserves punishment. Pedestrians have as much right on the crossing as any vehicle, though many drivers do not appear to think so."

* * *

"To loaf about street corners and in doorways will prove an expensive luxury hereafter", warns the *Victoria Warder* of Thursday, March 1, 1877, in reporting a new by-law against street loafers.

On March 15th the *Warder* said: "The Street Inspector was on the lookout for loafers on Sunday last. As he knows nearly every young man in town, it will not do for them to stand at corners

An early club in Lindsay was the O.R.B. club and many youths who were later to become eminent citizens were members.

until he approaches and then make off . . . he knows the name and that is all he requires." Breaches of the by-law would be heard in police court, said the editor. On March 22nd, the newspaper noted briefly: "Street loafers are still numerous!"

* * *

Doctors and dentists advertised regularly for customers in the columns of early Canadian newspapers. In the *Lindsay Advocate (and County of Victoria General Advertiser)* published in Lindsay, Canada West by E. D. Hand on Saturday, May 26th, 1866, a one-column, one inch display advertisement reads: "Dr. Fidler, surgeon to the Gaol! and Coroner."

A William Burnett, Surgeon Dentist, late of Toronto advertises that he is now in business in rooms over Knowlson and Gregory's drug store, corner of Kent and William Streets: "All operations known to the profession performed in the most satisfactory manner."

A Dr. Ingersoll, graduate of Queen's University, Kingston, C.W., and late surgeon, U.S. Army, advertises his office in the McDonnell's building: "Advice and recipes furnished *gratuitously to the poor* every Wednesday and Saturday from 10 a.m . to 1 p.m."

* * *

The *Lindsay Advocate* of May 26th, 1866 announces the dissolution of the partnership of John Knowlson and Edmund Gregory of the firm of Knowlson and Gregory, Druggists and Seedsmen of the town of Lindsay. The business was carried on by Edmund Gregory and today Gregory's drug store is still in business, at the same location, and still owned by the Gregory family. It is the oldest drug store in North America still operated by the same family.

* * *

The issue of *The Canadian Post* for Friday, February 27th, 1891 reports on the federal election campaigns in North Victoria Riding.

The Post, a Liberal newspaper and a supporter of candidate John A. Barron, comments on his opponent Sam Hughes (then the editor of the *Victoria Warder* and later Canada's Minister of Militia in World War One):

> *Wherever he (Barron) goes his good humour and urbanity as well as his arguments increase his already great popularity while Sam Hughes is making a fool of himself, as usual, by his slanderous attacks on his opponents, his irritability and splenetic utterances.*
>
> *At Balsover, the other evening, Mr. Jonathan Folliotte, a well-known and respected resident of the vicinity, and a local preacher, asked Mr. Hughes what he would do about the prohibition petition now in circulation. Sam tried to avoid giving a direct answer by saying he had not made up his mind as to what he would do; but upon being pressed by Mr. Folliotte, at last said: 'Show me the petition, and I'll tell you in ten seconds what I'll do.' As Mr. Folliotte had not got the petition and could not show it, the matter dropped; but next day in Kirkfield it was spoken of, and Mr. Hughes cooly remarked, with his usual disregard for consequences, that Mr. Folliotte was a 'slippery Methodist and a d----d hypocrite!'*
>
> *Anywhere and everywhere, in print and out of it, Mr. Barron's self-constituted opponent is the same old unsavoury Sam, heaping insult and abuse on all who offend him.*

The *Post* article claimed that a long time ago, when Sam Hughes came to Lindsay, he tried to buy *The Post*, and finding it was not for sale, but that *The Warder* was, purchased the *Victoria Warder* and turned Tory. "And it turns out that what we had heard was perfectly true," wrote the *Post* Editor.

* * *

The following advertisement in rhyme appears in *The Canadian Post* for Friday, September 12th, 1861:

BOVARIUM

Good Meat I keep, as all do know,
  Adjoining Joseph Funk's
The flies, I warrant, do not "blow"
  Upon my tender junks.

Beef, Mutton, Lamb and Veal also
  In season you will find;
And, if of soup you want "a go",
  Speak for the tails in time.

Good Marrow-bone, Kidneys likewise,
  Sweet-breads and Tit-Bits all,
Livers and Tongues; — if you are wise,
  You'll soon give me a call.

Lindsay, Sept. 5th, 1861.   —NED MORRIS

* * *

Before *The Post* building was built on William Street, a Mrs. Pigott conducted a business on the site and one had to go down a step in order to enter her little frame store. The youngsters of those days used to tantalize the woman by shouting through the keyhole.

The proprietress used to sell a concoction known as "choke dog", later given the name of Victoria Pie. This was a mixture of everything in the pastry line and was baked in a large pan and topped off with a thick crust. It was very popular with the young people and a few coins would buy a large slice.

* * *

The *Canadian Post* in its issue of Thursday, October 1st, 1863, comments on its contemporary, *The Lindsay Herald:*

> The editor of the Lindsay Herald pouts that we have not given him a word of advice or encouragement on the 'circumstance of a new luminary bursting forth in the newspaper

heaven!!! Ye gods and little fishes, isn't that splendiferous! Now, since it is quite evident from this alone, that our Tory neighbour, and more, his chum the Advocate, will never set the Scugog on fire, we say to him DON'T publish a newspaper — drawing teeth is better.

* * *

The *Victoria Warder* of May 3rd, 1877 records that at an "informal meeting" a request of the Victoria Railway presented by Mr. James Ross to grant a right-of-way down William Street was refused. It was decided that the Victoria Avenue route would cause "less damage and injury to the town."

* * *

On November 10th, 1876 "the Great Original and Renowned General Tom Thumb and his wife" appeared at the Opera House, Lindsay, for two performances. General admission was twenty-two cents, children under ten years paid fifteen cents and reserved seats were priced at fifty cents for adults and twenty-five cents for children.

* * *

The following poem, entitled "The Editor" was printed in *The Canadian Post*, April 5th, 1877:

> "*Scratch, scratch, scratch for*
>   *his daily bread,*
> *The editor sits with low, bent head;*
> *He writes that the rest of the world*
>   *may read*
> *That old man Jones has made a deed,*
> *Or that little John Smith had stole*
>   *a pig;*
> *That farmer Black from earth has passed.*
> *Thus he writes of all that is said,*
> *Till at last we hear that the*
>   *editor's dead,*
> *Rest has come for the weary hand;*
> *He held free tickets for the better land.*

Declaration of Twinning

The Town of Lindsay, Ontario Canada

The City of Nayoro, Hokkaido Japan

By His Worship John F. Eakins

Whereas the council of the Corporation of the Town of Lindsay, on the Seventh day of July, in the year 1969, did resolve to declare the Town officially twinned with

Nayoro City, Hokkaido, Japan

And Whereas Mayor Kohturo Ikeda of Nayoro City has proposed a sister-community relationship be established between his city and Lindsay, and marked on and from the First day of August in the year 1969,

Now, Therefore I, John F. Eakins, of the Town of Lindsay, hereby declare that as from Friday, the First day of August, in the year 1969, Lindsay is twinned with Nayoro, whereby, we citizens pledge to observe and uphold a sister-community relationship, and to join in the pursuit of peace, justice, and friendly co-operation in a manner which will make each of our communities windows towards international understanding. To demonstrate this, we shall, on civic occasions, fly at our Town Hall, the Flag of Japan alongside the Flag of Canada.

And Whereas representative citizens of Japan have this day attended in Lindsay to participate in the twinning of Nayoro and Lindsay,

And Whereas the citizens of Lindsay and Nayoro share a mutual desire to foster an exchange of education and culture in art, religion, industry, economics, agriculture, politics and sports.

Now, Therefore I declare that the Town of Lindsay, Ontario, Canada, is officially twinned with Nayoro City, Hokkaido, Japan.

August 1, 1969 Town Hall, Lindsay, Ontario, Canada

Signed: Mayor, John F. Eakins

Witnessed By Members of Lindsay Town Council

Original Declaration of Twinning signed by Mayor John F. Eakins and Council, 1st August, 1969.

The "Glorious Twelfth"

The "glorious Twelfth", Queen Victoria's Birthday and Dominion Day were three occasions for merry-making in Ontario a hundred years ago.

A report of one boisterous "twelfth" celebration by Orangemen drew some caustic comment from the *Canadian Post* of Lindsay, and in turn the *Post's* editorial brought a retort from its contemporary the *Victoria Warder*.

The *Canadian Post* editor wrote in his edition of July 22nd, 1870:

"The *Warder*, with its usual stupidity, falls foul of our reporter's brief notice of the 'Twelfth' of July, because the report was not couched in the elegant and perspicuous language which our *confrere* always affects. It ill becomes the *Warder*, who lately *suppressed* an important motion passed at the town council, because its publication might place some of his friends in an awkward position, to charge us with inaccurate comments on the proceedings of the 'Twelfth.'

"Besides, he knows very well that we never charged, nor never contemplated charging the Orangemen with 'rowdy' or disorderly conduct — *that* feature of the case has existence only in his own diseased imagination. The immense crowd of Orangemen who visited Lindsay on the 12th were respectable and most orderly — but after all there were a number of parties drunk and there were 'a couple of free fights'. All this is quite compatible with strict sobriety and quietness on the part of the Orangemen — although their would-be-organist can't see it."

Again on July 29th, 1870 the *Post* took another little dig at the *Warder* editor.

"The *Warder* accuses us of making an effort to 'secure the patronage of the Roman Catholics of the country.' Nothing of the kind. We do not seek the 'patronage' of any denomination or soc-

48

Views of parade and ceremonial arch — probably Orangemen.

iety, as such. But we could, with far greater propriety, charge our *confrere* with 'bidding' for Orange support, from the nonsensical position he has taken in connection with our notice of the 'Twelfth'.

"He still holds that the paragraph was 'insulting and untruthful,' but fails to show where the insult or the untruth comes in. This style of treating a subject is peculiar to the *Warder,* and therefore does not surprise us. The old aphorism certainly holds good in his case — 'convince a fool against his will, and he'll be of the same opinion still.' "

The *Warder* again replied with an editorial titled "The Post and the Orangemen" in its issue of Wednesday, July 29th, 1870:

"We clip the following precious paragraph from the *Post's* 'Interesting' and *truthful* account of the celebration of the Twefth in Lindsay.

" 'During the day we observed a number who had indulged rather heavily in something stronger than soda water, and were forced to succumb to the dire influence of "sunstroke"; a couple of free fights were also indulged in, caused by two intimate acquaintances with "Old Rye" — the participants were properly taken care of, and rooms secured for them at No. 1 *Palace de la Rue,* Market Square, and thus ended the celebration of the "glorious Twelfth" in Lindsay.'

"Now anyone reading the above would be led to believe that we had a very 'rowdy' celebration, when the fact is, that a more respectable body of men never marched through our town. This is not the first time our *confrere* has put forth such inuendoes, nor is it the first time we have been called upon to notice his mean attacks on the Order, for it will be remembered that two years since, he paid the Orangemen a similar compliment; but considering the source from whence such attacks come, perhaps we attach too much importance to his veracity to notice it farther."

The editorial attacks between the conservative *Victoria Warder* and the liberal *Canadian Post* went on for decades. Watson Kirkconnell in his fine book "County of Victoria Centennial History" published in 1921 and issued in a revised, updated edition in 1967, wrote: ". . . the local press indulged in orgies of Billingsgate probably unique in the annals of Canadian journalism."

An editorial in the *Victoria Warder*, Wednesday, April 27th, 1870, states: "Any person in the habit of reading the *Canadian Post*, cannot but notice the persistent cowardly attacks made on Mr. Whalley by the individual who does the dirty work of that slandering journal. There is hardly a week passes that there is not some attack made upon him without the shadow of a cause . . .

"The supposed writer in the *Post* never meets a charge; he acts like a boy behind a fence, who throws dirt on the passers-by, and then either runs away or denies the act." Mr. Whalley was apparently an insurance agent and an editor of *The Warder*.

The "Billingsgate" reached its height during the years Sam Hughes was the editor of *The Warder* and Charles D. Barr, former night editor of the *Toronto Globe*, was editor of *The Canadian Post*.

Hughes wrote in an editorial, addressed to his contemporary at *The Post:* "Long before I came to this country, your reputation was established as a kind of editorial bully and blackguard. Now you stand exposed and discredited. Like the mongrel cur fit only to annoy nobler things, always, sneaking, howling, dodging kicks, and when caught, cringing and whining, the object at once of pity and contempt; you have long held an unenviable position in the esteem of your fellow townsmen."

Continuing in this vein for some time, Hughes concluded: "Truly sir, you are a despicable wretch. Like the detestable insect, fearing the light of day, biting in the dark, whose touch is loathsome, you also are an object of disgust. For the future see, if it is not too late, to become even an excuse for a man . . ."

The office of Victoria Loan and Savings Company is now the office of Frost, Frost and Gorwill.

Historical plaque commemorates the naturalist Ernest Thompson Seton. From left: John Childs, Jasper Forman, Arthur Burridge, Dan McQuarrie, Rev. Orville Locke, Leslie M. Frost, Lloyd Found.

Time Capsule in Cornerstone

When the cornerstone of the present St. Paul's Anglican Church in Lindsay was laid on Dominion Day, 1885, a scroll, coins and newspapers of the day were placed in a metal box and sealed into the cornerstone area of the building.

The text of the scroll reads:

In the name and by the favour of Almighty God, the glorious architect of heaven and earth, on the first day of July, and the era of Free Masonry, in the forty-ninth year of the reign of our gracious sovereign, Victoria, Queen of Great Britain, Ireland and the dependencies of Europe, Asia, Africa, Australia, the Dominion of Canada, Empress of India, etc., his excellency, the Most. Hon. the Marquis of Lansdowne, being governor-general of the Dominion of Canada; the Hon. John Beverly Robinson, being lieutenant-governor of Ontario; and the Rt. Hon. Sir John A. Macdonald, C.C.B., etc., etc., premier of the Dominion of Canada; the Hon. Oliver Mowat, Q.C., premier of the province of Ontario; J. R. Dundas, esq., M.P. South Riding of Victoria; J. W. Wallace, esq., mayor of town of Lindsay; M.W. Bro. Hugh Murray, grand master, Grand Lodge of Canada; the Rt. Rev. Arthur Sweatmen, D.D., Lord Bishop of the Diocese of Toronto; the Rev. S. Weston-Jones, incumbent of the parish of Lindsay; Robert Bryans, esq., and Adam Hudspeth esq., Q.C., churchwardens; A. Hudspeth, Robert Bryans, Wm. Grace, Thos. Walters, D. Browne, building committee; Messrs. Stewart and Denison, architects; Messrs. McNeely and Walters, Builders.

The cornerstone of St. Paul's Church was laid by Most Worshipful Bro. Hugh Murray, grand master, Grand Lodge of Canada, assisted by the officers of the Grand Lodge and a large concourse of the brethren in accordance with the customs and usage of the order, which may the C.A.O.T.U. ever protect and prosper.

There is contained in the vessel to be deposited in the cavity of the stone: A copy of the proceedings of the diocese of Ontario for 1885; Dominion Churchman; Evangelical Churchman; Daily Mail; Daily Globe; Canadian Post; Victoria Warder; an historical sketch of St. Paul's Church; Canadian coins of the denomination of 50c, 25c, 10c, 5c and 1c.

The original St. Paul's was built in 1859 on a grant of one acre of land on the south side of Kent Street. This was a large frame structure, built on the site of the old post office, now the site of the Dominion Store.

Prior to this, regular meetings were being held since 1855 in the town hall.

The earliest records for Lindsay, then known as Purdy's Mills, go back to November 26th, 1836, when the Rev. T. C. Wade preached at Mr. Rea's residence (Reaboro) in the township of Ops, about twelve miles from town.

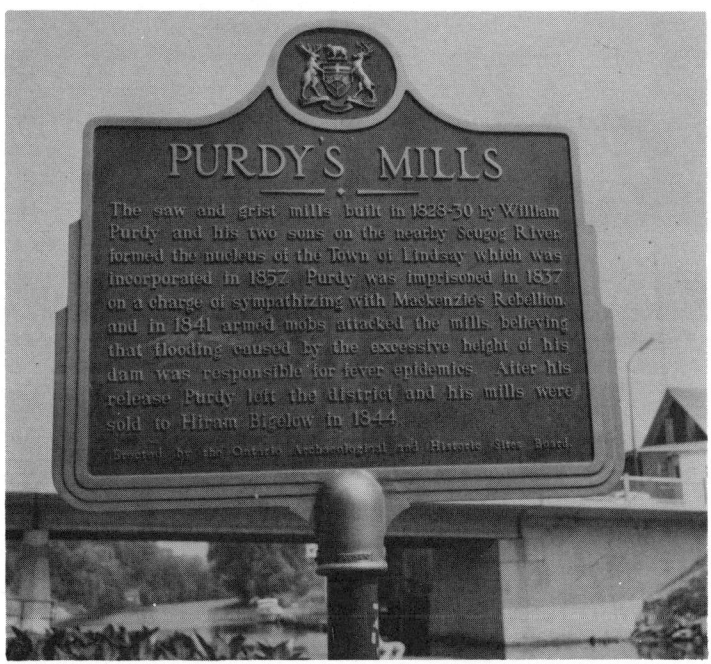

This view of the Scugog River at Mcdonnell Park shows approximately the location of the original Purdy's Mills. The provincial archeological and historic sites board plaque marking the founding of the town stands in this park.

Visit of Billy Sunday

Over fifty years ago Billy Sunday, the U.S. evangelist who preached of hellfire and the effects of demon rum, called on people to "hit the sawdust trail" in Lindsay.

William Ashley Sunday (Billy Sunday was his real name) was a Fundamentalist. He was ordained in the Presbyterian Church in 1903.

Despite his sensationalism Sunday was enthusiastically received by the evangelical churches and by influential laymen. He played a prominent part in the prohibition movement and was at the peak of his fame in 1917 at his New York City revival. Born in 1862, he died at Chicago, Illinois, on November 6th, 1935.

A Lindsay newspaper gave an account of one of his Lindsay rallies that was well attended.

"A rapid firing gun is Billy Sunday, the evangelist . . . a machine gun that hurls a perfect fusillade of bullets at the enemy. So rapidly flows the mountain torment of his eloquence that at times the words trip one another up. The willowy form is in constant motion; he runs rapidly from one end of the platform to the other, leaning far forward to shake his finger, or clench his fist at the audience; at other times doubling up like a jack-knife.

"Sometimes in his excitement he stands up on one foot, using the other leg as well as both arms for gesticulations; an interesting talker, sometimes a whirlwind of sarcasm and invective.

"He goes after the rum power not so much with new arguments as with new phrases, new gestures, perhaps new enthusiasm. He is sensational and dramatic, at times almost grotesque. Thus he falls on the floor in order to describe a drunkard falling.

"Billy Sunday lived up to the maxim that he who would first move others must himself first be moved. The sweat runs down his face and drips to the floor."

The newspaper report called Billy Sunday's rally the opening gun in the temperance campaign to have Ontario dry by Dominion Day, 1916.

Many Newspapers have served Lindsay

Lindsay's first newspaper was published by Edward D. Hand, a short, vigorous and bearded man who also established two other newspapers in Victoria County.

Mr. Hand was born in London, England in 1832 and came to Canada in 1851 at the age of nineteen. He worked in Port Hope for a couple of years before entering the employ of the *Port Hope Guide*.

In 1854 he moved to Lindsay and established the first newspaper in the town, *The Lindsay Advocate*. It was sub-titled "And County of Victoria General Advertiser."

The newspaper carried on its front page the slogan "Extremes are generally errors; the truth usually lies between."

The paper was published weekly from his office at Knowlson's rough-cast block, Kent Street, and advertising rates and subscriptions were quoted in sterling. The job printing department offered every kind of plain and ornamental job printing "executed in a style equal to that of a country office and at moderate prices."

By 1858 Mr. Hand had a competitor, according to advertisements in the 1858 Directory of the United Counties of Peterborough and Victoria, "The Victoria Herald and General Advertiser", published by H. J. Waite on William Street. No copies of this newspaper appear to have survived.

By 1861, the year of the great fire, the town had three newspapers, the *Lindsay Advocate*, the *Lindsay Herald* and the *Canadian Post*. The *Post* had moved into Lindsay from Beaverton just before the fire and was being published by C. Blackett Robinson. The *Omemee Warder*, was still in Omemee at this time. It was shortly to move to Lindsay as the *Victoria Warder*.

Three weekly newspapers in a town of 2,000 was at least one too many and the *Canadian Post* purchased the *Lindsay Advocate* about 1866, sent the presses and equipment to Orillia with foreman Peter Murray and on May 3rd, 1867, on the former presses

LINDSAY ADVERTISEMENTS.

The Lindsay Advocate
AND
VICTORIA ADVERTISER
IS PUBLISHED EVERY THURSDAY,
By E. D. HAND,
AT HIS OFFICE, UP-STAIRS IN KNOWLSON'S BRICK BLOCK,
KENT STREET, LINDSAY.

Terms: 5s. per annum in advance; 10s if not so paid.

EVERY DESCRIPTION OF PLAIN AND ORNAMENTAL

JOB PRINTING.

Thomas Broughall's Cash Store,
Knowlson's Brick Building (Centre Shop),

STAPLE AND FANCY DRY GOODS,
CLOTHING AND MILLINERY.

☞ Great Bargains always on hand.—Country produce taken for Goods.
Corner of Kent and William Streets.

---

of the *Advocate*, the first edition of the *Expositor and North Simcoe Journal of the Times* appeared.

Following the sale, Mr. Hand moved to Bobcaygeon and founded the *Bobcaygeon Independent* in 1870. A few years later he sold it to Charles Russell Stewart (1826-1905) who had come from England to Canada as an agent for the Canadian Land and Emigration Company in 1862.

Next, Mr. Hand moved to Fenelon Falls and founded the *Fenelon Falls Gazette* about 1872 and he continued to publish this until his death on March 17th, 1919, at the age of eighty-seven years.

This photograph of the block at the corner of Lindsay Street North and Kent Street was taken around 1864, or later. It shows a Music Emporium, the *Canadian Post* printing house, the Post Office and Charles Britton's law chambers. To the left was an office of the *Canadian Post*, and the Piano and Organ store appears to have been operated by an A. M. Reekie.

The weekly *Metcalfe Warder* commenced under the ownership of Joseph Cooper and Joseph Twell in 1856, became the *Omemee Warder* in 1857 when the village changed its name, and moved to Lindsay as the *Victoria Warder* in 1866.

The Lindsay Herald was a short-lived paper as was *The Lindsay Expositor*, published in 1869. A weekly *Lindsay News-Item* was published by Sam Porter for a few weeks in 1895 and *The Lindsay Free Press* was published for a short time in 1908-9.

C. Blackett Robinson, who brought the *Canadian Post* to Lindsay from Beaverton in 1861, sold the newspaper in 1862 and he started the *Whitby Gazette*. He found competition against the long-established *Whitby Chronicle* difficult and when one of the two *Post* partners of George Cruickshank and John Duff Wallace (operating under the title of G. Cruickshank and Co.) decided to return to Scotland, Mr. Robinson again took over *The Post*. This was in the early spring of 1864.

He was in partnership with Thos. C. Bartholomew for some time, but a notice in the *Post* in July, 1870, announces the partnership of C. Blackett Robinson and Thos. C. Bartholomew dissolved and the newspaper and general print shop continued under the style and form of C. Blackett Robinson.

In 1870 Mr. Robinson moved to Toronto and founded the *Canadian Presbyterian*, leaving *The Post* in charge of his brother-in-law, George T. Gurnett, until 1873 when Charles D. Barr, night editor of the Toronto Globe, took it over.

In 1888, *The Watchman* was established by Joseph Cooper and in 1899 George Lytle bought the *Watchman* and the *Victoria Warder* amalgamating the two of them as *The Watchman-Warder*.

The *Warder* also published a daily edition for a short time in 1908-20 and again about 1938-9. In April, 1940 the newspaper was sold to S. R. Pitts by J. W. Deyell.

The Watchman-Warder was closed out in recent years after well over one hundred years of publishing, while *The Lindsay Daily Post* continues the name and traditions of *The Canadian Post*.

The *Canadian Post's* daily edition, then named the *Evening Post*, was started by George H. Wilson of Port Hope in 1895. Since the 1930's his son Roy P. Wilson, has been publisher and proprietor of the company.

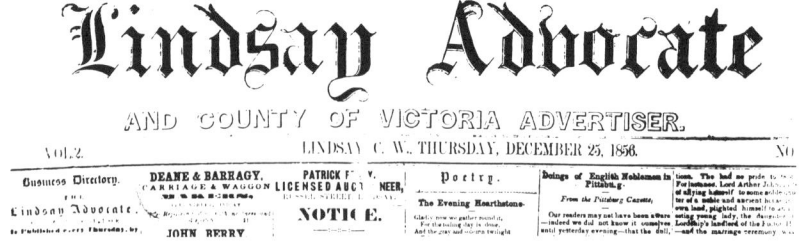

Masthead of *Lindsay Advocate*

THE EVENING POST

LARGEST CIRCULATION OF ANY TOWN DAILY PAPER IN ONTARIO.

LINDSAY, ONT., MONDAY, NOVEMBER 11th, 1918.   Established 1893.   2c Per Copy.

VICTORY!

"Praise God From Whom All Blessings Flow"

Germany Signs Armistice
Triumph For Democracy

TERMS OF THE ARMISTICE ARE HERE OUTLINED

KAISER BILL FLED TO HOLLAND — DUTCH AUTHORITIES ARE UNEASY

LONDON, Nov. 11.—4.45 a.m.—The arrival of William Hohenzollern, the former German Emperor, with his wife and oldest son, has caused excitement and much uneasiness among Dutch authorities and public of that country, says a despatch to the Telegraph from Rotterdam. It is unofficially stated that the refugees did not obtain authorization from Holland to enter the country and crossed the frontier in the neighborhood of Eysden beside the Dutch neutrality guards were weak at that point.

TORONTO, Nov. 11.—The call for demobilization of Germany's army, surrender of part of her fleet and dismantling of the rest, are the terse announcements of the State Department. It did not tell anything of the scenes at Marshal Foch's headquarters at the time the armistice was signed. It was stated, however, that at five o'clock (Paris time) the signature of Germany's delegates was secured to document, which blasted forever two dreams which once ruled the world in a struggle which had cost at the very lowest estimate ten million lives.

PARIS, Nov. 11—(9.06 a.m.)—Prussian ministry at Hamburg has been arrested at his home in that city according to Basel despatch.

WHEN GOOD NEWS CAME

The news of the signing of the armistice was telephoned to The Post from Toronto at 2.26 o'clock this morning, and later telephone messages are confirmed it. At 4.46 o'clock The Post received word from C nadian Press Association and His Worship Mayor Kylie was notified. The 'phone has been kept busy ever since.

The Post is issuing a war edition to-day and in this hour of jubilation our readers will feel sure will overlook the absence of local and other news.

"Make a joyful noise unto the Lord, all the earth make a loud noise, and rejoice, and sing praise. Sing unto the Lord with the harp, with trumpets and sound of cornet. Make a joyful noise before the Lord, the King."
Psalm 98

FOCH LEFT NO LOOP HOLE FOR HUNS TO RESUME HOSTILITIES

(Special Post Service.)
WASHINGTON, Nov. 11.—Kaiser Wilhelm has fled to Near Utrecht, Holland, according to a German press report reaching this Government this afternoon.

WASHINGTON, Nov. 11.—At six o'clock this morning (U.S. Eastern time) the greatest war in history came to an end. The State Department officially announced early to-day that German plenipotentiaries signed the United States-Allied armistice terms at Foch's headquarters at five o'clock this morning and that hostilities ceased at 11 o'clock, (both French time). While an armistice merely halts war and does not end it, the terms laid down by Foch are such as to prevent Germany from renewing hostilities. The war, therefore, may be regarded as definitely over.

There remains now the great problem of the Peace Conference and the work of returning the fighters to their home land. As to the first, Geneva and Brussels are mentioned as the most likely points; for the second the General Staff already has completed its plans for demobilization. At the close of the unprecedented strife Germany stood alone, before the wrath of twenty-two civilized nations. Those twenty-two were in arms, five others had severed relations with her government, and two others—Russia and Roumania—she embittered by enforcement of a vicious peace. Her enemies had called to the colors twenty-three million men during the conflict, determined to crush forever the power that held up the peace of the world. Her allies, Bulgaria, Turkey and Austria-Hungary had left her when her strength began to weaken and finally her own people, seeing at last the disaster their treacherous Emperor and War Lord had brought upon them, overthrew his reign and he has fled the country. In the kaleidoscopic events of the four years of war, twenty-four great nations participated in the fighting. Over thirty million men were under arms. More than sixteen million were killed, wounded or gassed. The war has cost more than one hundred billions of dollars.

The actual terms had not been announced by the State Department up to early to-day. Word apparently was awaited from Paris as to any possible changes in phraseology at the Foch Headquarters at the last moment. The text, as shaped by Versailles Conference, was in possession of the State Department, and it was assumed that it would be made public during the forenoon.

The terms were strong. They were such that Germany could not renew the war even if she would. They made it certain that the associated supremacy should be assured. That was scarcely necessary, for Germany was thoroughly defeated in the field, and the crack in morale at the Somme had written "finish" on the struggle long before the document was signed.

WASHINGTON, Nov. 11.—Germany signed to-day an armistice agreement that branded her before the world a beaten nation. By its terms she surrendered in the field to a better force than the mighty military machine her autocrats had built. By it she agreed to evacuation of occupied territories. She swore away her hold on a generous portion of her battleships and submarine fleets. She acceded to demands for surrender of a portion of her war material. In other words she admitted that the Allies were victorious, and agreed to a strong stipulation which made the nation unable to remove the strife even if the shattered people were so inclined.

PERIOD GIVEN FOR EVACUATION EXTENDED TO TWENTY-FOUR HOURS

WASHINGTON, Nov. 11.—The momentous news that the armistice had been signed was telephoned to the White House for transmission to the President a few minutes before it was given to the newspaper correspondents. Later it was said that there would be no statement from the White House at this time.

LONDON, Nov. 11.—5.40 a.m.—The period given for evacuation of the left bank of the Rhine by German forces has been extended by twenty four hours, according to French wireless despatch received here.

WASHINGTON, Nov. 11.—The world war ended at six o'clock this morning, (Washington time) with red revolution in Germany and with William Hohenzollern, former Emperor, fugitive from his native land. Announcement of armistice terms imposed by Allied and American governments had been signed by German envoys at midnight last night (five o'clock Paris time) and that hostilities would cease six hours later, came to the State Department at 2.45 o'clock a.m. The terms of the surrender of Germany were not made public coincident with this announcement, but they were to be given out later in the day. The momentous news of the ending of war was given to newspaper correspondents verbally by an official of the State Department.

COPENHAGEN, Nov. 11.—Hesse-Darmstadt has declared itself a Free Socialist Republic, until German Republic is established. The garrison at Dresden is in hands of Provisional Soldiers and Workmen's Council.

CANADIANS CAPTURED MONS

LONDON, Nov. 11.—To Canadian troops fell the honor of capturing the last important town before armistice put an end, Mons, where the British made a brilliant stand at beginning of war, was regained early this morning by Canadians.

"O sing unto the Lord a new song; for He hath done marvellous things; His right hand and His holy arm hath gotten Him the victory"
Psalm 98

The front page of the *Evening Post* for Monday, November 11th, 1918, showing how the residents of Lindsay read of the armistice. "Praise God from whom all blessings flow" read the line under the banner heading of Victory!

My Home Town

Lindsay's first Old Home Week was held June 28th to July 5th, 1924. A song "My Home Town" was written for the occasion by W. W. Staples and C. R. Ashman and put to music by W. C. Forsyth. The words of the song read:

There's music in the very name
Of my home town,
Somehow, the folks seem different there,
Maybe it's something in the air,—
I know the flowers are far more fair
In my home town.
In memory oft I journey back
To my home town,
Where shadows creep and lights are low,
Old visions haunt me—and I go
In fancy to the ones I know,
In my home town.
What do I find when I go back
To my home town?
Ghost faces of the past I see,
A story written round each tree,
Old friends in dreams to welcome me
To my home town.
There's no place I would rather be,
Than my home town.
Whether the years have brought me fame
Or failure—yet in Lindsay's name
They smile and greet me just the same,
In my home town.
Old friends are best (I've tried the rest);
In my home town;
Please let me live, just for one day
Let me go back, and hear them say
"We've missed you since you've been away,
From your home town."

Builder of Railways founded Hospital

James Ross, who founded the Ross Memorial Hospital in Lindsay in memory of his parents, was born in Cromarty, Scotland in 1848. He was the son of Capt. John Ross, a merchant and shipowner.

He came to Canada in 1868 as an engineer and was involved in the construction of the Victoria Railway. William Mackenzie, another man famous for speedy railway construction, worked with him on the Victoria Railway.

Ross was an outstanding construction engineer and Mackenzie (who had been born in 1849 at Kirkfield, Ontario) and Donald Mann (born in 1853 at Acton, Ontario, and one time a resident of Fenelon Falls) worked with Ross on the construction of the Credit Valley Railway.

In 1886 Ross came east to build the Canadian Pacific Short Line across Maine and again Mackenzie and Mann had contracts connected with the line.

Later James Ross joined Mackenzie in the Toronto Street Railway enterprise and they were also involved in street railway systems in Montreal, Saint John and Birmingham, England.

He also built railways in Saskatchewan and elsewhere in Canada, and Col. Sam Steele of the Royal North-West Mounted Police in his book "Forty Years in Canada, Reminiscences of the Great North-West" published in 1915, wrote of Ross, "he was regarded by the leading contractors as the ablest manager of construction they had ever known."

For some years prior to 1878 James Ross lived in Lindsay and it was here that his son J. K. L. Ross was born. His parents John and Mary Ross also lived in Lindsay for a number of years.

A story is told, which may be legend, of the origin of the hospital. Some years before the town had a hospital, Judge G. H. Hopkins who had a law practice in Lindsay (later of Bayuga) found a man lying ill on the sidewalk on William Street south. Mr. Hopkins arranged for a room in the Maunder House Hotel and saw to it that the man received medical attention.

Mr. Hopkins later related his experience to a Mr. Paddon, then manger of the Bank of Montreal, and in the company was Mrs. James Grace, sister of James Ross who was to found the hospital.

After listening to the story of the sick man, Mrs. Grace said her brother had expressed the wish to build a hospital in memory of his mother and father.

This incident led to the founding of the hospital and to the act of the provincial parliament, legalizing the gift of the hospital to the board of governors which was passed on January 9th, 1903.

On January 12th, 1911, the nurses' home near the hospital was opened and named the "Annie Ross Nurses' Home" in honour of James Ross' wife who died in 1915.

In his will Ross, who died in 1912 in Montreal, left the hospital another legacy.

Many expansions took place at the Ross Memorial Hospital over the years. The Victoria maternity wing was added in 1929 and an extensive new wing followed in 1957.

In the past two years all the buildings, with the exception of the new wing, were pulled down and replaced with a modern new structure that will continue to serve the citizens of Lindsay well as the "Ross Memorial Hospital," perpetuating the name of one of Canada's leading railway builders.

The first Board of Governors of the Hospital comprised the following: Chairman J. D. Flavelle; secretary-treasurer J. R. McNeillie; directors John Austin, George Ingle, Thomas Stewart, Robert Bryans and Mrs. J. C. Grace.

Squire McDonnell

The beautiful park and rock garden beside the Scugog River is known as McDonnell Park, but it might have been known by some other name if Mayor R. M. Beal, had had his way in July, 1915.

The park had been named for "Squire" William McDonnell, an eminent local political and military figure. McDonnell's house, somewhat altered, is now the home of Branch 67, Royal Canadian Legion.

The question of renaming the park came up at a council meeting in 1915. Mayor Beal said he did not favour having town parks named for people. He said he had the same objection to the name McDonnell Park as he would have to calling it Beal Park.

The mayor looked with favour on the name "Riverdale" or "River View Park", and Alderman Smale suggested that it be renamed to commemorate some notable battle fought in the First World War.

Council decided to leave the park as "McDonnell" for the time being and it was never changed in name. But for a few town aldermen it could have been renamed Riverview or Vimy Ridge Park.

A provincial plaque commemorating the founding of Purdy's Mills is erected in the park.

William McDonnell was mayor of Lindsay in 1864. He had first come to Lindsay from Peterborough at the head of a militia company that he had raised when it had been reported that some sympathizers of the Mackenzie Rebellion were in Lindsay seeking recruits.

McDonnell is credited with having taken the first census in Victoria County, being appointed Census Commissioner by a warrant issued January 2nd, 1852. He was one of the first Justices of the Peace for the District and in 1857 he was appointed Surveyor in Her Majesty's Customs at Lindsay, a position he held for a number of years. He was a Lieutenant-Colonel in the militia.

He was chairman of the old Lindsay grammar school board and was active in municipal affairs.

Born in 1814 at Cork, Ireland, he died in 1900.

The Squire McDonnell house, now part of the Royal Canadian Legion, is shown in a view from the Scugog River around 1890. To the right of the picture is the area that is now part of McDonnell Park. St. Andrew's Presbyterian Church can be seen in the background. William McDonnell paid his first visit to Lindsay in 1837 at the head of a militia company, raised to investigate rumours that members of the Mackenzie rebellion were in Lindsay seeking recruits. He was a justice of the peace and from 1857 was Surveyor of Her Majesty's Customs at Lindsay. (Photo from negative owned by Phil Polito, Lindsay.)

Getting back at Col. Sam

Lt.-Gen. Sir Sam Hughes (1853-1921) of Lindsay, when militia colonel of the 45th Victoria Regiment and a member of parliament, offered unilaterally, in 1898, to raise and command a battalion of men to serve in the Sudan under Lord Kitchener. When the South African war came, Hughes once again was impatient to get in the fight despite the opposition expressed by Major-General E. T. H. Hutton, an Imperial officer in command of the Canadian forces.

The upstart militia colonel eventually managed to get himself to South Africa and the stories of his exploits there consist of a fantastic mixture of fact and apocrypha.

Col. Hughes sent back a number of private letters to Canada and some of these boastful and political letters were printed without his permission in a Toronto newspaper. The actions of the relative in giving the letters to the newspaper was bitterly resented by Hughes.

The *Lindsay Post*, a Liberal newspaper that opposed Hughes, published a travesty on Sam Hughes' war letters and the following is from a copy reprinted in the *Peterborough Review* on Friday, April 13th, 1900, entitled "Getting Back at Col. Sam."

Modder River, 30th Feb., 1900

To the Editor of the Post.

Dear Sir — As many of your readers — notwithstanding their political misfortunes — are interested in my career as a soldier and military correspondent, and one who can supply upon the shortest notice the most startling war news, I take this opportunity of advising you and them of some of the more notable of my exploits since my arrival in South Africa.

You have been surprised no doubt at the absence of my name from the despatches, but then, you know me of old, and also my blushing coyness, and retiring bashfulness which, while they have always formed one of the most pleasing and obtrusively apparent of my characteristics, have at the same time always stood in my way. Me and Roberts have had high words over this, he insisting, and I refusing, to have my many acts of reckless daring recorded in the despatches. There is not the same objection to my mentioning them to you, as your paper has no circulation in the Transvaal and it does not seem like boasting. To you, therefore, I shall make a clean breast of it, and at the same time state nothing but the bold facts.

I relieved Kimberley, I captured Cronje, I reduced Bloemfontein — that is, me and Roberts — or "Bobs" as I generally now call him. "Call me 'Bobs,' Sam" says he. "To tell you the truth, Roberts," says I, "I don't like to get too familiar on short acquaintance — that's where me and this here Hutton had our split. You will recollect I pointed out to him that the British troops of today were not worth their salt, and that the Yankees, if they got at them, would mop the floor with them. Then he gets quite sassey, as if it wasn't for his own good. But then, you are different, and I don't mind if I do call you 'Bobs'." So Bobs it has been ever since.

You heard of Joubert's death. The Pretoria papers report that he died of stomach trouble. That is all rot, and like their Boer impudence in trying to conceal the truth. The fact was that he heard of my advance and succumbed to heart failure. His last words were "I'd rather die — Hughes is coming! Oh! my suffering country." Pathetic, isn't it.

I have frequently asked "Bobs" to let me tackle the Boers singlehanded, but he always makes excuses, looks confused, and tries to put me off. I would just say here that while "Bobs" is a most deserving officer in his own small way, and will do good work as long as I am with him, he lacks those great conversational powers and that pluck, and dash, and finish, which are only to be acquired by having had untrammelled sway and supreme command of the Victoria Volunteers. Just a word in your ear — he knows that my tackling the Boers would mean the ending of the war, and he is in no hurry to give up his present job.

"Bobs" said to me the other day (he is fond of quoting Latin) "the eyes of Vox Populi are upon us." This means in

This picture, dated 1911, shows Mayor R. M. Beal of Lindsay reading an address of welcome to Col. Sam Hughes on his return to town after being named Minister of Militia in the cabinet of Prime Minister Sir Robert Borden. On the box of the horse-drawn carriage (wearing a high hat) is Hunter Trotter; left on the bandstand: I. Earnest Weldon, Mayor R. M. Beal, Col. Sam Hughes, John Carew, MPP and Joseph Brown. On the far right in uniform is Fred Holmes, Officer Commanding the 45th Regiment. At the time this picture was taken the Armoury had not been built and the terrace at the left was later torn down to provide a site for the building. (Photo from the late Art Beal.)

common language that everybody is looking. "Sam", says Bobs to me the other day with a smile, "Sam, why are you like Sampson?" "I don't know" — says I — "because I am of powerful assistance to you?" "Well, not alone that," says he. "Why, then," says I. "Because," says Bobs, with a smile, "because you perform your greatest exploits with the jawbone of an ass." I don't see the point of this joke myself, but it just shows you how familiar we have become.

I am writing this from Settle's tent where I am in supreme command of the army mules — Yours from the Tented Field.
          SAMBO LONGBOW STRONG BOW HUGHES.

(For those whose history is a little rusty, Roberts or "Bobs" is Field-Marshal Earl Roberts, V.C., a distinguished British soldier who took over in South Africa in December, 1899, and entirely reversed the unhappy military situation there before handing over command to Field-Marshal Earl Kitchener a year later. Sam Hughes was later to become the Canadian minister of militia in Sir Robert Borden's government in the first World War.)

Bogus plates hidden in Walls

When the former Logie house on the Verulam Road was demolished in 1963 four metal plates were found fastened by wires from the attic and hidden between the walls.

These plates had apparently been used to print counterfeit money at the turn of the century. The plates would produce bogus banknotes of the period when individual banks issued their own currency. Both sets of plates represented $5 bill denominations, one dated January 2nd, 1895 and the other 1900.

The counterfeit plates described as "excellent" were confiscated by the Royal Canadian Mounted Police.

About the turn of the century Robert and Henry Logie were jailed for passing counterfeit bills.

The *Fenelon Falls Gazette* of October 12th, 1900 records the receipt of a bogus quarter at its office when a bill was changed and it was reported that other bogus quarters and bogus half-dollars had turned up in the village. "If they all resemble the one we saw," wrote the editor, "they are poor imitations of the genuine coins and can be detected at a glance as well as by 'ringing'.

"Anyone who inadvertently takes one, and doesn't know from whom he got it, should destroy it at once, as it is against the law to knowingly pass bad money, even though good value has been given for it."

Mayors of the Town of Lindsay

Robert Lang, 1857, 1859-61;
James McKibben and William Thornhill, 1858;
Thomas Keenan, 1862-63, 1865;
William McDonnell, 1864;
A. Lacourse, 1866-68;
David Brown, 1869-70;
George Downer, 1871-72;
John Dobson, 1873;
L. McGuire, 1874-75;
Thomas W. Poole, 1876-77;
Col. James Deacon, 1878-80; 1886;
F. C. Taylor, 1881-82;
J. W. Wallace, 1883-85;
Thomas Walters, 1887-90;
Robert Smyth, 1891, 1896-1900;
Duncan Ray, 1892-93, 1905;
Henry Walters, 1894-95;
George Ingle, 1901-02;
J. J. Sootheran, 1903-04;
Dr. A. E. Vrooman, 1906-07;
James B. Begg, 1908-10;
R. M. Beal, 1911, 1913-15;
Dr. J. W. Wood, 1912;
D. J. McLean, 1916;
Richard Kylie, 1916-18;
B. L. McLean, 1919-20;
John O'Reilly, 1921-22;
F. J. Carew, 1923;
W. G. Graham, 1924-25;
Thomas Wilkinson, 1926-27;
Col. R. Ivan Moore, 1928-29, 1949;
W. Eric Stewart, 1930;

Samuel Alcorn, 1931-32;
Frank Armstrong, 1933-34;
Percival E. Pickering, 1935;
Cecil G. Frost, 1936;
Dr. H. D. Logan, 1937;
A. T. Claxton, 1938-41;
Charles Lamb, 1942-48, 1950-53;
Albert E. Hick, 1954-57;
J. Lloyd Burrows, 1958-60;
Joseph C. Holtom, 1961-65;
John F. Eakins, 1966-1971;
H. David Logan, 1972-

* * *

Bobby Gimby plays "Ca-na-da" in Lindsay with school children during Centennial Year.

John Boyd has been a photographer for over twenty-eight years specializing in portraits, architectural and commercial photography. He started his profession at Panda Photography, Toronto, in 1946 and then worked with Paul Rockett in Toronto later returning to Panda.

He opened his own studio in Lindsay in 1957 with a partner, Robert Payne. John and Bob operated Kenlin Studio until 1970 when John Boyd and Associates Studio was opened.

Lindsay Portraits
by John E. Boyd

Gloria Barrett

Ford Magnes

Walter Humphries

Hattie Bate & Al Kirk (Little Theatre)

Norman Ryckman

Moe Wileman

Charles Heels

Frank Weldon

Alan Roy Capon of Picton, Ontario is the Managing Editor of The Picton Gazette. He was born in Ipswich, Suffolk, England and came to Canada in 1957 working for CKLY Radio, Lindsay, was publisher of The Minden Progress, editor of The Lindsay Daily Post, Lindsay Bureau Chief for The Peterborough Examiner and Prince Edward County Bureau Chief for The Whig-Standard of Kingston. He is the author of "His Faults Lie Gently", a biography of the incredible Sam Hughes and "Stories of Prince Edward County".